ABRAHAM
LEARNING TO TRUST GOD

REDEMPTION THROUGH GOD'S RIDICULOUS MERCY

RALPH CORDUAN

Abundance Books

Abraham: Learning to Trust God
Redemption Through God's Ridiculous Mercy Series
Copyright © 2025 Ralph Corduan
ISBN: 978-1-963377-46-0

Published by Abundance Books, LLC
Kalamazoo, MI
abundance-books.com

Interior and Cover Designs by Taryn Golliher

10 9 8 7 6 5 4 3 2 1

Printed in the United State of America

"What a relief that we're saved and sustained by God's trustworthiness, not ours. Even so, we can find ourselves going back and forth when it comes to trusting God. This delightful series of reflections on the life of Abraham reminds us that, amid our foibles and frustrations, God's got us."

—DANIEL MCCOY, Ph.D.
Editorial Director of RENEW.org

"Portable, encouraging, and relatable reflection on life and the life of Abraham from the author's Christian perspective."

—BEN TURNBILL
Reasonable Faith Midwest Chapters Director

"In a world and culture that presses on all sides to perform and live our best life, it's easy for Christians to forget who our God is and allow fear and doubt to govern our thoughts and decisions. When the road looks uncertain, and regret looms, we attempt to steer our lives apart from God, which inevitably steals joy, harbors fear, and clouds the truth that God is always sovereign, and always good. Ralph Corduan points us back to Scripture; to the simple truth and reality of who God is, and who we are not. His journey takes you through Scripture to learn and remember to relearn how much God loves us and has a plan for each of our lives. *Abraham: Learning to Trust God* is relatable and encourages you to yield, reflect, and return to the safe place of trusting God."

—DR. ALANA ARGUELLO, DMin Apologetics
Author & Apologist at www.sovereignandgood.org

"Ralph Corduan is very insightful in this book about Abraham. As Christians, we all struggle at some point with the issue of completely trusting God in every aspect of our lives. Ralph brings out the fact that 'Abraham was a real man, as real as you and me. Real in every way including doubts, fears, victories, laughter, joy, anger – and the list goes on and on. He was also not a perfect man.' Proof that God can use us even with all our flaws. In the end, hope prevails as he points our minds and hearts back to our need to trust God in everything."

—RICHARD SUMMERFORD
Co-founder and former Associate Director of Child Evangelism Fellowship USA

"On the whole, the endorsement of an author by his brother may be suspect as to its objectivity. However, the story that Ralph Corduan tells in this book is a personal one, relating the story of Abraham to his own life, and thereby to all of us in our shared humanity, including his brothers. He frames a picture of our inability to fix our own lives by mapping out blueprints for God to follow and our frustration when God has other plans for us. Still, when we look more closely at what God is doing in our lives, we find his grace and what Ralph has called God's Ridiculous Mercy. If your life is bigger and more complex than you can handle on your own (and if you're human that will always be the case), reflect with Ralph on what it means for us to really trust our Lord."

—WINFRIED CORDUAN, Ph.D.
Former Professor of Philosophy and Religion at Taylor University
Author of several books including *A Reasonable Faith: Basic Christian Apologetics* and *Neighboring Faiths: A Christian Introduction to World Religions*

CONTENTS

A NOTE FROM THE AUTHOR

We will focus our attention primarily on the life of Abraham. His name was Abram and his wife's name was Sarai before God changed their names. For ease of reading, I will remain consistent calling him Abraham and calling his wife Sarah.

Ralph Corduan

INTRODUCTION:
THE QUESTION OF TRUST

Can you really trust God? It's a fair question. The controversy surrounding it is magnificent. How can one person say "yes" and another say "no"? From my perspective, God has disappointed me many times, and yet I believe He is trustworthy. Quite a dichotomy, huh? Add to that this thought: The pews in our old churches and the chairs in our modern churches are filled with saints who are not radically convinced of God's trustworthiness. Really? How can I possibly say that?

Let me explain.

We trust God for our eternity (which we cannot see) but become squeamish about the light bill (which we can see). We trust God to build a mansion for us in heaven (which we cannot see) while being envious of the boss's new car (which we can see). That inconsistency is mind-boggling. I am not pointing fingers; I am describing my life. Therefore, my goal in this study is to address the conflict between trust and mistrust. I want to share with you what I have learned regarding God's redemption through His ridiculous mercy.

Through the years of getting to know God–through the ups and downs—I have learned the hard way to trust Him. I have found hope, encouragement, and help in God worth sharing. We can't see the future. We don't know what lies ahead. But God has the overview and sees our eternal good. That is more important to Him than our temporary comfort.

What you are about to read probes a little deeper into the paragraphs above, and some thoughts may surprise you. The following are portions of my life's trail as a follower of Jesus—a child of God. Thank you for coming along.

CHAPTER ONE
TRUSTING GOD

The sun slipped into the horizon as I rolled the vacuum over the office floors. The life my wife and I knew stood on a ledge of thrilling chaos and adventure. Hopes and dreams, anticipation and imagination put pep into my work. Humming, I emptied wastebaskets and freshened restrooms in the office building where I worked. A vibration on my belt indicated a new message on my pager. Finding the nearest phone in the office down the hall, I punched in my home number. I heard the familiar voice shout with excitement on the other end. "I think it's time!" My heart skipped a beat.

"I'll be right there!" I yelled and slammed the receiver down. Darting toward the door, I tripped over a yet untouched wastebasket, spilling papers, soda cans, and a leftover banana peel all over the used-to-be clean floor. Sidestepping the mess, I kept going. My foot slid on the carpet, and I smashed my leg into the corner of a desk.

"Arrghh!" I screamed while rubbing my sore knee.

Limping, I reached the exit and made several frantic attempts to push or pull the door open. Why isn't this opening? This shouldn't be so hard! How does this thing work again? The mystery was somehow resolved, and I made it out the door.

Stumbling through the entrance into the adjacent police station, I panted and screamed, "Brad? BRAD!"

My best friend rushed around the corner in his uniform.

"Brad...Water broke...It's time...Gotta go...Get baby...Need hospital... This is it."

He grabbed his keys and chuckled, "Okay, let's go get your wife."

Screaming sirens and flashing red lights pierced the darkness when we arrived at the apartment in record time to pick up my soon-not-to-be pregnant wife.

My thoughts ran wild. Boy or girl? Who cares as long as the baby is healthy and has ten fingers and ten toes? Hmmm, it is ten, isn't it? Come on, of course it is. Why am I so giddy?

In the birthing room, the nurses came in and out, measuring, poking, and prodding. The fetal heart monitor was a constant reminder of the new life getting ready for roll call. Suddenly, the steady beeps picked up speed and began to send rapid warning signals.

The doctor pulled me aside. "Her labor has stalled. The baby is in distress. Our only option is to perform a c-section."

I shook my head. How did we go from "Honey, it'll be fine," to "There is a problem?"

The doctor looked at me and spoke. His flat voice puzzled me, "We need to prep her now." The team of nurses mechanically began the routine procedure for yet another c-section while my world was collapsing.

My stomach turned sour. A whirlwind of thoughts kept pace with my racing heart. No, this cannot be happening.

The medical staff seemed immune to my distress and steadily circled around my wife like honeybees buzzing around the queen.

"You can't be in the operating room," the doctor told me in an attempt to rush past me. He was a cantankerous man who acted like he had drawn the short straw because he had to work that day, or any day. Skilled in his field, we learned to ignore his bedside manners which resembled a cornered mama bear keeping intruders away from her cubs.

Undeterred, I pleaded and argued relentlessly.

"You may not enter!"

"I will not leave my wife," I responded.

"You have to."

"But I won't!"

"You can't!"

"I will."

Finally, it became apparent he could go home sooner if we stopped debating. With a scowl, he nodded and allowed me to be present for the procedure. Once inside the sterile room, his confident demeanor instilled complete trust.

The surgical team moved like one being. Their actions, smooth on the surface, but deep and powerful underneath—like a wide river moving through a grand mountain meadow. In no time my wife was prepped for surgery.

Then, all the buzzing, beeping, and commanding orders from medical staff and doctors became muffled.

I blinked. I couldn't believe what I saw.

A spring-loaded tiny little arm with an open-handed wave exploded out of my wife's belly right after the doctor cut through the skin and tissue. This "Hi" sign, to me, a just about brand-new daddy, linked our hearts together and solidified our bond from that point on.

I rocked back and forth on my heels, excitement bubbling from every cell in my body. I felt like I might jump out of my skin. Our baby waved at me before he was even born!

Everything seemed to move in slow motion as our tiny little package was placed in his mamma's arms. We had a beautiful and healthy baby boy. My eyes welled up. I understood for the first time a father's great love for his son. Little did I know this laid the anticipation for what, at the time, was incomprehensible: the love of the Father for His Son.

I beamed, grateful to witness God's incredible handiwork of the creation of life.

Suddenly, everything changed.

Less than an hour old, our son's body was too still.

He had stopped breathing.

I swallowed hard.

A nurse whisked our baby from my wife's arms. In an instant, the other side of the room filled with nurses and medics. My hands trembled. My legs wanted to give way. The gruff voice behind our doctor's surgical mask told me to leave the operating room.

I returned his steely glare. Six wild horses could not have removed me from that room.

"Please, God, let him live," I begged.

God must have heard me. Moments later, I heard our son wail a strong cry—more delightful than the clasp of thunder after a long drought. God's ridiculous mercy!

Tears slid down my cheeks into my mask. I released a breath of air trapped in my lungs. My emotions felt like puppets on a roller coaster.

During those few minutes of total helplessness, I knew I could do nothing. I was forced to trust in someone else, someone with the wisdom, training, and knowledge I did not possess—the medical staff.

Thankfully, our boy experienced no complications from the few minutes without oxygen.

I do not believe in coincidences. God knew who He was entrusting this child to. That team of competent medical staff was placed in that hospital on the day of my son's birth.

Nowadays, he is a grown man with his own babies, and I'm still in awe of God.

I look back on that defining moment and often wonder if Abraham felt as I did the first time he saw his son. What about later, when Isaac lay on the altar? Did Abraham also feel the world stop as mine did when he faced the imminent loss of his son's life? What thoughts ran through his mind as he, in complete obedience, raised that blade above Isaac to offer him as a sacrifice to the great Jehovah?

Life and death, or other similarly significant events, seem to mark decisive moments in our time on this side of eternity. They can shape our worldview and even change the trajectory of our lives.

For me, those pivotal moments were starter lessons about trusting God. And learn them I did. Well… some. I still have a lot of learning ahead of me. Parents and children should be on a learning, teaching and trusting adventure. This fundamental relationship between father and son is designed to transfer to our relationship with God.

As we know, trust is fundamental to any healthy relationship. We might desire others to depend on us. It is a compliment and an honor to be sought out by someone to be their confidant or to be entrusted with a treasure for safekeeping. Conversely, it would hurt if we overheard somebody say we were untrustworthy. Broken trust, whether it's in business or with friends or family, can be devastating.

Unfortunately, we have all offended someone. Sometimes, we realize it, and other times, we are completely oblivious. The Bible says we should ask for forgiveness when we realize our offense. We have a choice. We can repent and ask for a second chance. Or we can also go in the other direction and justify our conduct. These opposing choices or actions depict a delicate battle. There is something humbling about admitting our wrongs. How often does pride get in the way of resolving conflicts?

Has someone broken your trust? Even as simple as not showing up for coffee or as impactful as blabbing something personal that was meant to be confidential? Memories like that, or others, can become pet rocks we stuff in our pockets, bulging, but neatly covered.

What about God? What happens when we believe God breaks our trust? Have you ever felt that way? Have you ever heard a friend or a colleague tell you, "I've tried the God thing"? Maybe they said they gave God a chance, but He didn't come through. What happens when God seems to let us down? Are we even allowed to ask such a terrible question? Is it sacrilege?

I do not believe God is intimidated by these questions. Are you familiar with the phrase 'stepping out in faith'? Often, this refers to an action beyond normal, rational thought, and involves relying on God rather than ourselves. Another way of saying it is to fully trust God. In my life, I have done this several times–in small moments and with major decisions—and several times fallen hard onto the steel floor of disappointment. Here are a few examples:

> One Christmas, I wanted to buy a new winter coat for my wife. Instead, God nudged me to give the money to a college student in my Bible study group so he could go home to visit his family. Did God let me down because He did not replenish the money?

> Standing in line behind a mother and her babies in a grocery store, I watched her fumble through her pockets to find enough money to buy her groceries. When I helped pay for her food, I needed to put some of my items back. Did God let me down because now I had less than I wanted?

> To this day, my mind often returns to the decision of leaving the security of a full-time income to pursue a vocation in ministry, only to have to go back to work again. Did God let me down because He did not provide the income?

Do I only trust God to give me back what I give Him? That sounds more like a business transaction than trust, doesn't it?

Is trusting God worth the risk?

I still have vivid imprints from middle school (God, please do this one thing for me) of revealing my deep love to the girl of my dreams. Her response was worse than finding out there was no Santa.

How many times did I ask God to heal one of my children of a recurring condition only to be met with hollow silence? You and I could list countless examples of frustrations. And so, I repeat my question: Do I only trust God when He does my bidding?

For me, it boils down to this—I want to be in charge, in control of my life. Why? Because I think I know better than anyone what will make me happy. From my perspective, God let me down several times. How, then, can I argue in favor of trusting God?

Trusting God is simple, but it isn't easy. I live in a constant tension of wanting to trust Him but not seeing the results I want. Sometimes, I feel alone, forgotten, and frustrated. Does that sound familiar? Do you, like me, struggle with trusting God?

The good news is that we are not alone. All the people in the Bible, the very ones we look up to, struggled just like we do. Abraham, a righteous man (Genesis 15:6) and a man of great faith (Hebrews 11) struggled with trusting God.

The very foundation of trust is knowledge of a person's character and historical facts. For example, I know I can always trust my few closest friends because of my history with them. They have stood by me through life's hardest moments when most people did not. That repeated behavior reinforces my trust in them.

Also, I know and trust gravity. When I jump up, I am confident I will not continue to float up, up and away and end up in outer space. And I trust that every time I take a breath, I will receive the oxygen my lungs need to breathe. Even though I can't see gravity and oxygen, I know they are both there, and I don't have to worry about them throughout the day.

God is the same way. Even though we can't see Him, we can know He is there. Every book in the Bible tells us so. We also know that He doesn't always give us what we want. Some wants are not ever realized; other times, they are delayed. Abraham, at seventy-five years old, waited for the next twenty-five years, torn between doubt and trust for his promised son, Isaac.

God is not a magic genie. He is, however, all-knowing, all-powerful, and all-present. As I have grown in my walk with God, like Abraham, I know God is trustworthy, despite what things look like in the natural world.

God is the only one who will never leave us, He will not turn His back on us. We can trust Him with everything we hold dear, including our children, our lives, and our eternal home. We serve not a god, but God. He will never change even though the world is continually fluctuating.

We touched a little on negotiating with God. Over the years I've managed to collect a whole arsenal of ways to motivate God, to bring Him around to my way of thinking. In the next chapter, I'll open my cache of tools.

TAKEAWAYS

1. Struggling to trust God is normal, healthy, and important in our walk with God.

2. We don't always get what we want; sometimes, we get something completely different.

3. We can trust God despite the circumstances.

NOTES

CHAPTER TWO
RIGHTEOUSNESS VS.
SELF-RIGHTEOUSNESS

Sunday after Sunday, I sacrificially served in my church. Dropping my hard-earned money into the collection plate, I leaned back in the pew and mused *You're doing pretty well, ole boy*; convinced I was a good Christian. I attended church even when I didn't feel like it. After all, how many Sundays did I sit through boring and meandering sermons and off-key worship sessions? In my mind, I was a pretty good dude, and silently thought God was lucky to have me on His team.

Through subtle deception, like many people, I negotiated a relative balance of a good versus bad image of myself. I compared myself to the worst of society and thought I was doing okay. How many think that if our good works for God outweigh our bad moments, St. Peter will open the Pearly Gates, and we'll get the ultimate prize: eternity in Heaven? That ideology creates tremendous pressure to be perfect.

What pressure or burden am I talking about? The greatest tension I imagine is, never knowing on what side of the balance beam we stand – good enough or below the mark. Consequently, that makes us susceptible to the exploitation of unscrupulous leaders. Given the right words combined with challenging life events, we might be motivated to perform on a subtle suggestion to gain favor with a whimsical god. (Notice the small "g". This is not the God of Abraham.) What a great system to manipulate people. The question is, can we put any stock at all into doing good works? Are any of us good enough?

We might even take that line of questioning a step further and ask, are we good enough for God to adopt us into His family?

For the majority of my life, I knew in my mind that the answer to that question was "No." I gave the stock answer readily when asked, but I didn't believe it in my heart. When I sinned, I felt crummy before God. On the other hand, when I read the Bible or witnessed to someone, I felt good before Him.

Some of us will admit we are not perfect but then justify our actions by asking, is anyone? The Bible tells us, "for all have sinned and fall short of the glory of God" (Romans 3:23).

I reckon that settles that question. Nobody is good enough.

These days I see how all my attempts to impress God were like soiled rags to my Savior. I can see all the so-called righteous things I did were just an illusion, an attempt to establish self-righteousness.

I am so very sorry. Sorry for my ignorance. Sorry for my misguided, intermittent enthusiasm. Sorry for my overall lack of understanding of God's ridiculous mercy.

The sin of self-righteousness plagues many of us, especially in the church. It's not attractive. Sometimes, I recognize how ugly it is when I see it in myself. But then, self-righteousness is tricky. It can camouflage and present itself as most humble while at the same time conveying superiority.

Don't we take it for granted that the way we look at things is the correct way? I can be pretty stubborn and dig in my heels. I often have thought or said, *my way is good (if not the best), and that's final.*

And if someone else has a different idea or opinion? The knee-jerk reaction is to convince them of <u>my</u> viewpoint.

My wife Lisa looks at things from a different perspective. She takes time to listen to others, applies biblical wisdom to the situation, and speaks the truth in love. I have learned to listen to her. How much more impactful is that concept when I realize that God may have, and often does, a different perspective from mine? It is absurd futility to convince Him of the superiority of my viewpoint.

If we truly understand that we cannot earn salvation through working our way into Heaven, why do we try to appease God with good works? Or try to make up for something we did or said that we know crossed a line with Him? Or why do we try to live a humble life attempting to impress God with our dedication to Him as if we can gain brownie points with the world's Creator?

We cannot perform or do anything to impress God to open wide the entrance door to Heaven. Some people act like they don't give it another thought. Maybe they truly don't care. Or is there an absence of fear of God in their hearts?

Others, like me, and possibly like you, ask, "Is it hopeless? Is there anything I can do?"

Great questions. And I have good news.

Nowhere in the New Testament is there a checklist or protocol for salvation that covers attire, length of hair, length of prayer, how to dress, frequency of baths, or other hygiene issues. There are also no limits on sins, levels of unforgiveness, education, heritage, or gender qualifications. (John 1:12, John 3:16, John 6:37, John 6:51, and many more verses make it plain that God's invitation is open to everyone. Anybody and everybody is welcome.)

It almost sounds like I am suggesting there are no requirements at all. Far from it. There is one; but only one requirement for eternal salvation. Simply stated, it is belief, trust, or reliance, if you will, in Jesus Christ, the Lord and Savior. That one act of faith completely changes us on both this side and the other side of eternity.

Sometimes, God calls us to an act of trust that truly tests us.

> *Now the LORD had said to Abram, "Get out of your country, from your family and from your father's house to a land that I will show you"*
> Genesis 12:1

I love that God simply shows up to talk to Abraham.

As we read this story in Genesis it looks like Abraham did what he was told. Or did he? More on that a little later.

At the time, Abraham lived in a town called Ur of the Chaldeans in Mesopotamia. What amazes me is that he is quite comfortable with God visiting and giving him a directive—leave your home and head to Canaan. There is no record of questions or debate. Abraham just took off. He became a wanderer, a nomad. Maybe this way of life was right up his alley. Perhaps God gave Abraham a restless demeanor to "go where no man has gone before." God chose Abraham. He knew he was the perfect man to set the stage for the great unfolding of His plan.

Abraham himself? Well, he was not so perfect.

We don't know much about Abraham's earlier life except that he was raised an idol-worshipping pagan (See Joshua 24:2). But then everything changed as God revealed Himself and spoke with him.

According to God's specific directive, Abraham was told to leave his home, family, and country and go to a land where God would send him. But did he? Did he leave his family? Not really. Abraham took his wife, Sarah, and his nephew Lot, his dad, his brothers, a few other family members, and all the people he and his father employed with him (See Genesis 12:5). Perhaps here we can see a little chink in Abraham's armor—obedience with a well-planned safety net. Before Abraham made it to Canaan, a drought forced him, along with the rest of the clan, to head toward Egypt.

When they entered Egypt, Abraham's trust went right out the window. Why? What would cause a faith hero like Abraham to abandon his trust in God? Well, looking a little deeper, it's as plain as the ears on a mule. The Bible gives us the answer--he feared for his life.

> *And it came to pass, when he was close to entering Egypt, that he said to Sarai his wife, "Indeed I know that you are a woman of beautiful countenance. Therefore, it will happen, when the Egyptians see you, that they will say, 'This is his wife'; and they will kill me, but they will let you live. Please say you are my sister, that it may be well with me for your sake, and that I may live because of you"*
>
> Genesis 12:11-13

True, Abraham set out to follow God's charge. Did he miss a cue only to end up in Pharaoh's court? Obviously, Pharaoh held the power over life and death. Maybe Abraham doubted God's power or doubted His ability to save him. Could Abraham trust God to protect him?

In obedience, Abraham took that first step of his journey that continued for over 2,000 miles. Amazing how time can wash away former firm convictions into obscurity.

I, too, have taken that first step in trusting God. Not just once, but many times. Then, step two, followed by step three, stumble a bit, and on to step four, and so on. By step fifty-two, I often wondered if I made the whole thing up. I toggled between rational logic and fragile faith. I would often question myself: What am I doing? I wonder, did Abraham do the same thing?

He had no control over the weather. The drought was not Abraham's fault. Whose fault was it? Isn't God in charge of the rain and the wind and the heat?

And now, to save his life, Abraham asked Sarah to tell Pharaoh she was his sister.

To understand this request, we need to get to know Abraham's family a bit better. He had a mother, a stepmother, his brothers Haran and Nahor, and his half-sister Sarah.

Haran, Abraham's brother, had a son, Lot, who later played a significant role in Abraham's life. Since Lot's dad died (Genesis 11:28), Abraham took on the father's role in Lot's life. Nahor and Sarah were his siblings by his stepmother.

As a side note, some have raised the question of incest at the marriage of Abraham and his half-sister. At the time all of this took place, the gene pool was not as contaminated as it is now, and marriage was common among family members. The practice didn't have the same genetic repercussions that it has now. Abraham used this sister-loophole to save his skin.

The Bible tells us that Sarah was a gorgeous woman. By entering this foreign land, Abraham, with good reason, feared Pharaoh would kill him to get Sarah into his harem.

Abraham trusted God to lead him this far, but how could God possibly protect him from Pharaoh? To save his own life, Abraham asked his wife to tell a half-truth or a half-lie. I understand. I want my life to be smooth, without hiccups. Like Abraham, I will look for a work-around when circumstances appear dicey.

Half-truths, just like half-lies, are used to deceive. Who is the author of deception and misdirection? Jesus tells us in Matthew 5:37 that we should say what we mean and mean what we say (paraphrased).

Let's remember it was not just Abraham who had a stake in this situation. Sarah faced the possibility of being ripped from her husband, never to see him again. I believe she loved and respected Abraham. And so she complied with his request and told Pharaoh she was Abraham's sister—not half-sister, nor his wife. This occurred near the beginning of Abraham's relationship with God.

Somehow, when things seem to misalign like that proverbial storm cloud forming on the horizon, we often feel we must come to God's rescue. We see the circumstances brewing around us with no sign of God's mighty hand intervening. If He doesn't jump in, what choice do we have? We must take matters into our own hands and help God out. Do we truly believe it's our job to come to His rescue, that He is helpless without us? Hmm, while our head shakes *no*, our actions may say otherwise.

I certainly felt this need to help God out in my aspirations of earning a living as a Christian musician. The exhilaration of the debut of my first CD was accompanied by a dismal success with bookings for concerts (I'll explain more later). "God, where are you?" When I didn't get the answer I wanted, I came to the same conclusion as Abraham. It was up to me to come up with a foolproof plan. I know, I'll release a second CD to create more depth as an artist. All I needed was a recording studio. What luck, we had an empty bedroom I could convert. I delved into soundproofing the new studio, with speakers worthy of accurate playback, instruments, sound effect processors, and a sixty-four-channel soundboard. I had plenty of time to record and mix due to the lack of bookings.

Hmm.

In full swing of helping God with my plan, I went all out and thought, wow, God must really want me to work on this project. No bookings yet. And then, He is really holding me back. And then, wow, nothing has happened yet. Still no bookings. I came to the conclusion success was obviously my responsibility, so I worked harder and longer hours. In hindsight, I can only apologize for my misplaced excitement. The idea that God had a different path for me never crossed my mind—until much later.

Helping God out may seem like a reasonable and commendable idea at the time, but trust me, God does not need our help. Now, I know and believe that.

Most of the time.

Except when I don't.

And then maybe some other times when He is really dragging His feet.

Like Abraham, I vacillated between trusting God and a fragile faith.

But back to our story at the gates of Egypt. Sarah ended up in Pharaoh's harem and now God had to come to Abraham and Sarah's rescue. He brought plagues into the king's household, and Pharaoh discovered the deception. Abraham got his wife back and an escort out of town. That was a close call. It would be logical to assume that from now on, Abraham walked the straight and narrow with God. Certainly, we expect this great man of God to act right. After all, he is in the Bible.

Did God choose Abraham because He knew He could count on him? At the very least, we would expect that once a lesson was taught, it was learned. Or was Abraham just like I am, and maybe, we are? As we continue this study, we will begin to answer that question.

But first, let's shift our focus from Abraham to ourselves.

How do we respond in uncertain circumstances? Do we not belong to the same God as Abraham? Can we or should we expect ourselves to act right?!

There have been seasons in my life when God overwhelmed me with something, and my response was, "I will never doubt Him again." Then … the next obstacle popped up—so much for my unabated trust.

I remember very well one instance of God's miraculous but very normal intervention in my life. My paycheck covered rent and beans, but not furniture. The bank account was slim, anorexic even. One evening, in a Bible study, a man walked in. He slept in his car, so I offered to share my barren paradise. A simple act of faith, trusting God would provide.

He did.

When I came home from work Monday evening, the apartment was fully furnished. For the first time, there was food in the fridge. I had no clue that the man I offered to help came from a wealthy family. His father was a multi-millionaire. I helped a stranger, and God poured out His mercy.

When my truck didn't start the next morning to go to work, I was in the same boat as Abraham again. God, where are You?

The good news is that we are in good company. No one in the Bible, except Jesus, is perfect. We are all flawed and need a Savior. That is why God sent Jesus. If Abraham needed God's help, what could possibly motivate us to think that we do not?

TAKEAWAYS

1. No one is perfect.

2. We all need a Savior.

3. God will always rescue us, but possibly not how we might want Him to.

NOTES

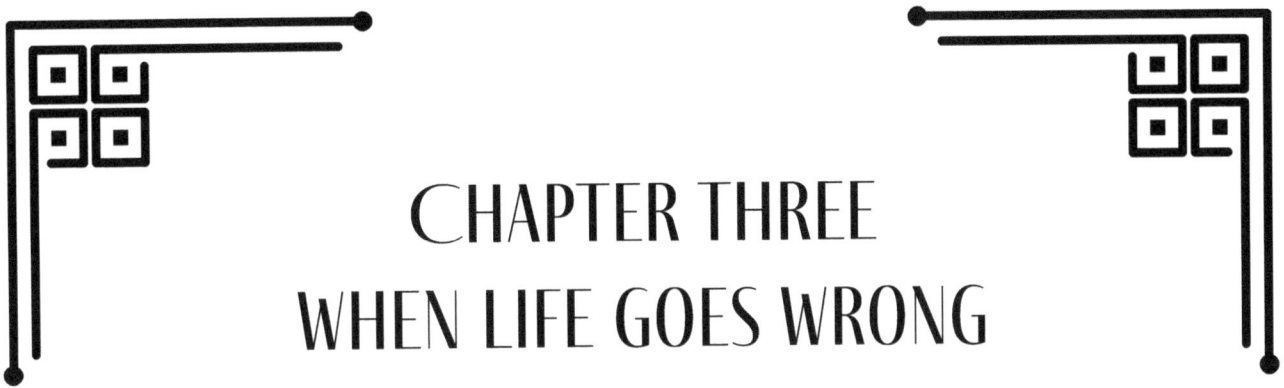

CHAPTER THREE
WHEN LIFE GOES WRONG

"God, are You sure? They created this position for me! I don't want them to think I am ungrateful." I questioned God's leading out loud in my prayer time.

Silence.

I persisted, "I do like this job, God, but I like singing more. Traveling the state and doing all kinds of repair work in all these places of business is okay. The job does pay well. I own all the tools in the back of the company van, got a company credit card in my wallet, that ain't bad." I informed Him as if He didn't already know.

My monologue continued, "Are You sure You want me to go into full-time ministry?" The tug-of-war between financial security and following a dream was real. I could think of nothing more fulfilling than living the life of a Christian musician. It was exciting.

Both Lisa and I were in perfect harmony regarding this next step in life, to take this enormous leap of faith. The months leading up to this were filled with prayer, counsel, hopes, planning, and fasting. We clearly felt all systems were GO!

Earlier that year, God allowed me to sign a record contract. Lisa and I both felt confident that bookings would soon fill up the calendar. We also had some savings to cover the first few months of expenses for our full-time Christian ministry.

All systems might have been set to go, but I went nowhere. I could not even get a booking at the local food shelter. If something didn't happen in the next few weeks, I would soon end up there, not as a guest singer, but as a resident.

I keenly felt the drought ahead of us. Abraham's drought was a lack of rain; mine was a lack of income. I lived in doubt with a generous helping of fear. The pantry echoed with silence and emptiness. How would we pay the light bill?

Don't you love hearing stories of how provision came just in the nick of time?

That was not the case for me.

The nightly conversations with my wife turned predictably to "What did we do? Did we misread the situation or the signs?"

She would respond compassionately, "Honey, we made the best decision we could with the information we had."

I knew that was true, but I still questioned our decision. *Should I have quit my job? Do you think the church we contacted last week will call back? If they do, that could be the start.*

Before long, that line of thinking became all-consuming. Whether sitting on the porch, driving along a country road, or at home on the couch, I couldn't think of anything else but self-doubt. More times than I can remember, my wonderful wife reached out and just held my hand.

"But what if nothing happens?" I would ask her. "We have friends in the pastorate. Can't God get through to them? Why isn't anyone responding to us?"

Leaning on me, my amazing wife reminded me to pray and continue to trust God. For a brief moment, I grasped a shadow of total trust, which faded as quickly as it appeared. These discussions became a loop for me as I rehearsed the same topic night after night. Laying there on the cold floor of disappointment, all kinds of lies plagued my mind: Am I a loser? Where is the all-powerful God who created heaven and earth? Does He even know I am here?

My mind continued to waffle back and forth as I reviewed the chain of events. The recording contract perfectly matched the timing. The counsel we received was overwhelmingly positive, except for one friend of more than 30 years. But my wife and I fully agreed about the decision to give up my lucrative job and step out in faith. My first concert was an overwhelming success. Then, the bottom seemed to fall out.

Did I misinterpret all the miraculous events and circumstances? Was God still in control?

Or did God use all these circumstances to align my path with His agenda?

When dark clouds settle around us during our faith-challenging times, isn't it good to know God already knows our thoughts?

Years later (as you know, hindsight is 20/20), I can tell you, and I can shout it across the valley: YES! YES, GOD IS IN FULL CONTROL! I could not see it at the time, but Plan B or happenstance is not part of God's vocabulary. Agenda surprises do not exist for Him.

Mercifully, like a patient, loving father, God gives us permission to wrestle with Him. I learned that following God does not necessarily play out like a movie. In those late-night discussions with Lisa, I learned God allows our lives to go sideways occasionally. My trust in Him was just as real as the doubt that followed. Strange, isn't it, how we can feed both doubt and trust at the same time?

After months of disappointment, I had to get a job. The company I resigned from could no longer hire an in-house maintenance man, but they were actively looking for a sub-contractor to perform those same tasks. They extended an offer to me, and I began my handyman business.

Through this business, Lisa and I reached people who would never darken the doorsteps of a church. God directed our steps toward what was good and turned it into something great. What I thought was a mistake was actually a much better plan for His Kingdom. God cares for His children through purposeful timing, direction, and leading.

> To everything there is a season, a time for every purpose under heaven. A time to be born, and a time to die; a time to plant, and a time to pluck what is planted; a time to kill, and a time to heal; a time to break down, and a time to build up; a time to weep, and a time to laugh; a time to mourn, and a time to dance; a time to cast away stones, and a time to gather stones; a time to embrace, and a time to refrain from embracing; a time to gain, and a time to lose; A time to keep, and a time to throw away; a time to tear, and a time to sew; a time to keep silence, and a time to speak; a time to love, and a time to hate; a time of war, and a time of peace.
>
> Ecclesiastes 3:1–8

None of these verses leave room for coincidence. Everything is under the control of the God of Creation. None of the detours, dead ends, and cul-de-sacs are mistakes, twists of fate, time wasters, or chance. God does and will direct the lives of His children.

As humans, we are not here by accident. You and I were born for this specific time, in our designated surroundings, and with certain talents. We are created on purpose. We are not a byproduct or accident.

There are some who want to convince us we are a fluke or a quirk of a cosmic alliance. In the attempt to avoid God, some theorize we evolved from amoebas, amphibians, or tomatoes.

God masterfully knitted each person together perfectly. You and I are fearfully and wonderfully made. The Bible confirms, "For you formed my inward parts; you knitted me together in my mother's womb" (Psalm 139:13 ESV).

When God formed each of us, I am sure He never mumbled, "I wonder what this will turn out to be?" He calls us marvelous (Psalm 139:14). Nothing in His creation is without thought and purpose. Even the earthworm has a job description. God made every living thing on earth.

Why is it that even those of us who know the omnipotent Creator as Father, still capitulate when life deals us lemons? Or a broken air conditioner in the middle of the summer? Or when things are totally out of control and we are scared?

Standing before Pharaoh, I can understand Abraham's panic, can't you?

In the face of fear, trust was no longer easy for him. Problems, hardships, or disappointments can push our trust off-kilter. When things get complicated, doubt becomes our best friend. Maybe Abraham asked some of the same questions I asked myself.

Should I have waited? Did I leave too soon? Was my timing wrong? Was the stage not yet set? Did I hear God correctly? I have raised these questions, not just once but often.

Going through my career-choice trial and looking in the mirror, I thought I saw Abraham's fearful eyes staring back at me. He faced Pharaoh. I had to face my friends, including my nay-saying friend who warned me not to quit my job.

Unlike Abraham, I didn't fear execution. I faced embarrassment, ridicule, and some snickering from those closest to me. Isn't it strange how much power someone's words or their approval can have over us?

During our difficult time, I repeatedly questioned God. I fell into the trap of thinking I wasn't good enough to deserve God's blessings. No way possible He could work any good out of my messy life.

The good news is we are not powerful enough to override God's plan for our lives. He even uses our mistakes and detours for our good and His glory (Romans 8:28).

How are you going to trust God during your faith-testing times?

TAKEAWAYS

1. We are not perfect—God is.

2. Have you ever heard this provocative phrase: "God has a wonderful plan for your life"? His perspective of what is wonderful may differ from ours.

3. God works all things out for good for His children.

NOTES

CHAPTER FOUR
LEANING ON GOD

"What?!" I stammered as I listened to the voicemail on my answering machine.

"I can't believe I didn't get that job! I am perfect for it!" I yelled into the pay phone.

The silence disagreed as the message ended.

I wanted to kick something as I trudged back to my truck. Slamming the door shut, I yelled, "God, help me, please! Where are you?"

The engine and I both hissed all the way home. Mercifully, I made it into the open parking space in front of my apartment. The sputtering truck painfully came to a full stop.

Frustrated, I jammed my key into the loose doorknob. As I tossed my keychain on the kitchen counter, I noticed a red light blinking on my weary, old answering machine. *Wait, did someone call after I checked my messages? Must be another job rejection.* That was the only thing this thing was good for anyway—recording rejections.

Reluctantly, I pressed play. *What?! Naw. Did I hear that correctly? Did someone just offer me a job?!*

For the next couple of minutes, I replayed the message over and over again.

I stopped for fear that I might wear out the incoming message tape.

Giddiness set in.

I finally had a job.

Thank you, God.

My cheeks started to hurt from smiling so much. This was cause for celebration. But where to? Of course, Taco Bell. They have the best dollar menu. Leaping out of my apartment and into my truck, I tried to turn the engine over, and ... nothing. I slammed my fists on the steering wheel. NO! No, no, no! NO!

Come on, God. I was just so thankful. Why this? Where are you? My trust and joy evaporated.

Eventually, with the help of a friend, I got my truck working. The next day, I rolled up to my new job. Taco Bell never welcomed me that night, and by now I was okay with that. My gratitude for the new job outweighed the loss of a plate of tacos.

Unbeknownst to me, God was teaching me by sowing seeds of gratitude into my heart, even when things didn't go as planned. This was a lesson I relearned years later when Lisa and I started our handyman business (remember chapter 3).

I wasn't the only one for whom God used setbacks and difficulties to build a stronger set of trust muscles. God did the same thing with our friend Abraham as He was building a closer relationship with him.

Do you recall God promised Abraham an offspring through Sarah? After a time, I'm sure this promise of a son was bathed in obscurity because Sarah was past her childbearing years. Reckon they thought, as an elderly couple, there was no way God's promise could come true without a little nudge from them. They formed a plan to continue his lineage through Sarah's handmaid, Hagar. A far-fetched plan for us, maybe, but customary in those times.

Hagar bore a son, and they named him Ishmael. The repercussions of that rescue mission (to help God) are still felt today. The descendants of Ishmael are modern-day Arabs. Muhammad is from the lineage of Ishmael.

But God had promised Abraham and Sarah a son, not Abraham and Hagar.

The promised child Sarah was to bear would be named Isaac. His descendants are the Jews whose homeland is Israel. The families of these two brothers, Isaac and Ishmael, are still at war today. Ishmael, Abraham's firstborn son, lost his birthright to Isaac. Isaac inherited all the accumulated wealth, cattle, and land, and he became the leader of the clan. That is the origin of this feud.

You can read about this not-so awesome plan Abraham and Sarah devised, in Genesis, chapter 16. The next chapter recorded the name change for the couple. Chapters 18 and 19 give us the account of Sodom and Gomorrah where Abraham interceded on Lot's behalf. But our story jumps ahead to chapter 20. I can't wait for you to read this.

Abraham's next recorded action encourages me more than you can imagine. Abraham, Sarah, and all their servants and livestock arrive in the land of Gerar with the reigning King Abimelech (Genesis 20:1-16). I would love to have witnessed the dialogue between these two men. You see, Abimelech's name means "my father is king," and Abraham means "the father of nations."

I can just imagine Abimelech, his voice dripping with scorn, asking, "Abraham, how many nations did you say you are king of?"

Abraham, clearing his throat, responded with a raspy, "Ah…er…none."

Bellowing with laughter, the king of Gerar seizes the opportunity to humiliate his new guest, asking, "And how many offspring do you have?"

"One," Abraham whispers.

Isaac had not been born yet, so, at this time, Abraham's only offspring was through Sarah's servant Hagar, not the son God had promised earlier.

When Abraham and Sarah did not trust God alone to make His promise a reality, we saw what their conclusion was, "We will just have to help God out a bit." Don't readily fault them, though; they could not read the Bible to see how it all turned out. They were in the middle of living and trying to figure out their life.

Just like we are, with one incredible difference, we have the Bible. We have a record of how God stood by His kids.

And yet, how often do we try to help out God because He's not moving fast enough? I know I can be guilty of this far too often.

Back to Abraham standing before this powerful king as a seemingly very small fish. I'm sure he feared for his life once again because of his beautiful wife. A common practice of that time was for the reigning king or ruler to kill the husbands of desirable women, take the women as possessions, and sometimes even marry them.

Funny how fear so quickly dissolves our faith. Once again, Abraham tells this king that Sarah is his sister. Maybe Abraham thought, *Well, it's partially true. After all, Sarah is my half-sister.* Even during that time, the status of marriage overrode the sibling relationship. Perhaps he thought, *What harm could it do? Everybody tells little white lies. That's just the way it is.*

And then, do you know what this powerful king did? Yup, Abimelech promptly whisks Sarah away to put her in his harem.

Earlier I said I found this encounter with Abimelech quite encouraging. By now, you might be asking yourself, isn't this the second time Abraham didn't trust God as he lied about Sarah being his wife? And why didn't Abraham learn anything, especially after all these years of walking with God?

Sometimes I wonder, *am I like Abraham?* Have I learned anything at all? It's like looking into a mirror, isn't it?

And that is exactly the point. Abraham is not different from us. He had to learn to trust God little by little, failure by failure. God knew Abraham, and God knows us.

Did Abraham really forget the first time God rescued him, in Egypt, from Pharaoh? When faced with a similar situation, Abraham and I suffer from the same affliction: divine amnesia. I forgot God's provision in the past during my seasons of unemployment.

How often do we need to repeat the same mistakes before we learn? I know for me, it can take some time as I repeat the same bad choices.

But God, with His ridiculous mercy, rescued Sarah unharmed from Abimelech. And then, years later, Abraham became the father of nations and multitudes through Sarah, just as God promised. It's incredible to look back and see God's faithfulness.

Sometimes, God purposely allows us to roller coaster down a bumpy road so we can grow our faith and learn to lean on Him despite our circumstances. It's during these times that we receive the confirmation that God is strong enough for us to lean on, even in the fiercest storm. Abraham witnessed this, and so do I throughout my rollercoaster ride of faith. Now I understand that if I hadn't gone through the tough times, I never would have personally comprehended the depth of God's love, provision, and protection of me.

TAKEAWAYS

1. When plans fail, it is easy to blame God.

2. God is still in control, even though you might not see it.

3. You can trust God despite the circumstances.

4. Look back over your life and see where God has been present.

NOTES

CHAPTER FIVE
GOD IS NEAR

"I totally blew it with God," my voice flat and hopeless.

Lisa and I met my brother, Win, one morning for a Bible study. He had always been the one I sought out when I needed straight answers to questions about the Bible or the Christian faith. The restaurant's dining room was wide open. Off in the back, a lonely, round, wobbly tabletop invited us to sit.

I love cheese on a toasted bagel, normally. This morning, not so much. Like foreshadowing of a bad novel, it was burnt. The cup of coffee proved to be more of a crutch in my hands than I realized. It cradled in my right hand, then the left, sometimes in both, never making it to my lips.

The discussion turned as uncomfortable as the hard, metal chairs. Squirming from side to side, I grew more and more unsettled, seeing where the conversation was headed. Nonchalantly at first, I referenced my failure of a life. And then the proverbial dam broke, as I spilled words and emotions I had only shared with Lisa until that morning.

"I have no clue how to make up for the shame I brought to God's name." I unraveled my hypocrisy of leading congregations in worship and leading youth groups in Bible studies while my home life was a disaster. Then came the divorce and the ugly truth of why my first marriage ended. Finally, I was given the left foot of fellowship from the local church. How could God ever welcome, much less use, someone like me in His kingdom?

Lisa gently laid her hand on my shoulder. Win listened, and I slowly gathered myself. My eyes stared at the cup of coffee that had somehow graduated from my hand to the table. He looked at me and asked one simple question, "What does light do?"

With the deer-in-the-headlight look, I stammered: "Ehhm, I guess it shines?"

"Exactly," he responded, "light is inherently bright and cannot help but shine." Slowly, the answer dawned on me.

"But as many as received Him, to them He gave the right to become children of God, to those who believe in His name" (John 1:12). I still believed Jesus paid for my sin. He had not rejected me. I was a sinner, yes, but a redeemed sinner.

I am a child of God!

After coming to terms and believing this one thing—Jesus paid the ticket for my/our sin—God takes over. We are His kids. Now His light is in us.

"You are the light of the world. A city that is set on a hill cannot be hidden" (Matthew 5:14).

God said I am light. A statement, a decree if you will, without any conditions attached. What a concept!

"Let your light so shine before men, that they may see your good works and glorify your Father in heaven" (Matthew 5:16).

Not too long after Jesus spoke those words, He paid for our sin with His life's blood. Read back over those words in Matthew again. We are the light. We don't need to strain to be light. We are!

Give that a moment to sink in.

As children of God, wherever we go, we are light. His light shining through us does not depend on how holy or rebellious we believe our lives to be at any given time or place.

God can use this sinner's life anytime. He can use any of us whenever and wherever He chooses. Sometimes, we like the circumstances, and other times, not so much.

It appears Abraham did not like his circumstances, walking through the land of Gerar. He feared King Abimelech. To save himself, he told a little white lie, a half-truth. But isn't the term half-truth just an avoidance of what it legitimately is—a deception?

Amazingly, God intervened and rescued Abraham and Sarah a second time. This man of faith trusted God and then failed to trust Him. How familiar is that? At times, I trust Him with my all and then with nothing at all. I wonder if you can relate.

Read on.

Wasn't Abraham the leader of the clan? Doesn't the New Testament call him a man of faith? How can someone like that fall so low? I find great hope in this because we hear of these great men of faith and jump to a conclusion that has a very present danger to flatten us.

We actually do believe, erroneously so, that these men of God were special. We seem to forget God is not partial to anyone. He did not create super-saints. Read these two verses.

"Then Peter opened his mouth and said, 'In truth I perceive that God shows no partiality'" (Acts 10:34).

And Paul writes, "For there is no partiality with God" (Romans 2:11).

Abraham fought the same battles we fight. Have you ever thought, If I would have seen the miracles the disciples saw ..., or If I had been there alongside Moses, slew the giant, or been called like Abraham, I would never doubt? Well, they were, and they doubted. God did not browbeat them. He allowed them to grow in their trust. It took years. We should not be discouraged or throw in the towel when we fail. We are in great company. The heroes failed and so will we.

"But God has chosen the foolish things of the world to put to shame the wise, and God has chosen the weak things of the world to put to shame the things which are mighty" (1 Corinthians 1:27).

Let's zero in on the last part of that verse. God chose the weak. From the beginning in Genesis to the ending in Revelation, the Bible is a transparent listing of man's weaknesses. It is okay to be or to feel like you are weak.

God uses failure-prone people, not only in history but also today. So, how do we qualify to be used by Him? Does He have a series of tests set up to weed out the not-so-useful from the very useful? Did Jesus leave behind a special tutorial or any hidden insight? No. I can only think of one prerequisite: believing Jesus is the Son of God who paid for our sins. The moment we believe, we are rescued from the power of darkness (often invisible to us) into God's kingdom of light (also often invisible to us).

I want to add an important side note here. James makes a statement in his letter that the demons believe God is one God. Believing Jesus paid for our sin is not a thumbs up or a mental affirmation. The entire spiritual world, good and evil, is convinced of who God, Jesus, and the Holy Spirit is. They know Jesus paid for our sin. When Paul said, "Believe on the Lord Jesus Christ, and you will be saved, you and your household" (Acts 16:31), it implies a desire for being delivered, rescued, or being made whole. Or to put it another way, there is a difference between believing in something and believing on something.

The thought of unseen kingdoms may not be foreign to us, but it is also not a common topic of discussion around a burger, fries, and a drink. We live in and see only the world around us.

Disabilities aside, every child born into this world, learns to depend on five senses. You smell the aroma of a home-cooked meal when your belly growls. You see the thin crispy skin of the Thanksgiving turkey just out of the oven. You risk an owie and grab the hot turkey leg. You hear your favorite aunt yell at you, just as you taste a big bite. Yum.

Hearing, seeing, touching, tasting, smelling. Are these the only senses required for life on earth?

"For we do not wrestle against flesh and blood, but against principalities, against powers, against the rulers of the darkness of this age, against spiritual hosts of wickedness in the heavenly places" (Ephesians 6:12).

Why bring this verse up? Who is involved in spiritual wrestling? Is it only the missionaries, preachers and evangelists? Does this verse involve our lives as well? We suspect there is more out there, but it is beyond our natural being—we just don't see it.

Because we do not see the spiritual beyond the tangible, most of the time it does not exist—in our mind. It is unnatural for us to see evil spirits manipulating everyday people to commit murder, slavery, perverse sexuality, deception, and so on.

And then we remember this often referred-to example about love: we cannot see it either, and yet it exists.

We do not see angels rescuing children from abuse, turning criminal husbands into loving leaders at home, or calling crooked politicians to honorable lives. We see the actions, not the cause behind the actions. We might not see what is behind the curtain, but spiritual warfare is real.

I am convinced we see only a portion of the life around us. Have you ever been in a situation or an environment where the hair on the back of your neck stands straight up for no tangible reason? I remember one instance several years ago when my son and I were walking through a mall. Into this store. Into that store. Searching for CD's, guitars, jeans, etc. My job was to make fun of the latest fashions and his was to call me old and out of touch. As we walked toward the entrance of the next shop, something stopped me. No doubt my son would laugh at me for what I was about to say, "Hey dude, I don't like this store. I get a weird feeling here." Shaking his head, he walked in, and I followed. There, on the rack in the back of the store, were colorful books inviting shoppers to flip through the pages. These books were geared towards teens with topics ranging from how to cast spells to how to entice the opposite sex to how to talk with your ancestors.

We know God has an enemy who wants nothing more than to turn us away from Him. What harm could it do to just flip through one of these booklets? Why is it that at the drop of a dime, our convictions and commitments, which we were once certain would never be challenged, are? How can we be so easily enticed? Don't be alarmed, everyone can relate to this. So, what did I do standing in the back of the store with my son? The hair on the back of my neck stood at attention. We needed to leave. Looking through the storefront window, "Wow, look at those pretzels at the kiosk! Do you want a plain one or almond covered?" For teenagers food is always a good distraction, and with that, I guided him out of the store.

Some folks talk about seeing angels or demons. I never have, that I know of. What I can tell you is my mind drew out an image of evil that day, clothed in pretty colors to woo unsuspecting souls and draw them into the pages of darkness.

When the bad guys show up—the enemies of God are out there—the good guys show up as well. You are not alone. Help is as close as the air around you.

"Are they not all ministering spirits sent forth to minister for those who will inherit salvation" (Hebrews 1:14)?

"For He shall give His angels charge over you, to keep you in all your ways" (Psalm 91:11).

We are not alone!

I'll say it again. We are not alone. When Abraham saw his life coming to an abrupt end in the presence of Pharaoh, and again with King Abimelech, he felt very much alone.

Abandoned by God.

How often do we feel alone and abandoned? We walk along, thinking all is well, never seeing the storm brewing that is about to take us out. But God saw Abraham's storm and He sees our storm. God is aware, and neither Abraham nor we are abandoned.

Read the verse below out loud.

"For I am persuaded that neither death nor life, nor angels nor principalities nor powers, nor things present nor things to come, nor height nor depth, nor any other created thing, shall be able to separate us from the love of God which is in Christ Jesus our Lord" (Romans 8:38-39).

God knows we need help. He did not just plop us on the ground with scribbles on a Post-it note that says, "Good luck!" He sees the battle we are most often not privy to. The powers, angels and principalities Paul refers to in Romans 8 are the bad guys, the evil spirits around all of us wanting to defeat us. The battle is for our souls, our spirits. God's angels, the good guys, stand guard over us to protect us and fight on our behalf. God knows we do not stand a chance left to our own strength or savvy.

Not only does He stand guard over us, but His Spirit is now inside of us-you know, the Light. It is a joy to be around some people, not because they are groovy or have some physical attribute we admire. I mean people who radiate God's character. Wherever I go, the light of His Glory is present and shines toward those I come into contact with. Not striving or forcing to shine and reflect God's heart, just walking through life as a redeemed child of His.

He knows we need outside help.

How do we get this outside help? Genesis 15 shows us this really obscure scene answering that question. Let's look at it next.

TAKEAWAYS

1. We may not see it, but the spiritual world around us sees the light inside of us.

2. God will not abandon us; we are not alone.

3. As a child of God, ponder the angelic protection detail surrounding you.

NOTES

CHAPTER SIX
GOD SEES OUR LIFE

"How long is this trail?"

"Are we ever gonna get there?"

Weary, defeated voices were muffled by the downpour that dampened our spirits as well as the trail. The campsite was hidden behind a curtain of rain until squishy footsteps suddenly gave way to "We're here."

But our relief, joy, and excitement soon collapsed into defeated voices: "It's all muddy, nothing but puddles of water. Now what?" I felt sixteen eyeballs focused on my dripping poncho, hoping for a miracle, waiting for instructions.

"Hang the backpacks on tree limbs, put ground cloths down, set your tents up as quickly as possible. This will be a night you will never forget!"

Before we knew it, amid grumbling and mounting tension, tents sprang up out of the ground. Afterwards, we huddled under the dripping leaf cover of the surrounding trees.

"Can we eat now?"

"So hungry."

The group of soon-to-be teenagers began clanking their pots and pans and firing their isobutane stoves. A concert of hissing and sizzling as the drops continued to drum on the flames gave way to the fragrance of the long-awaited evening meal. The mood soon changed to, "Mmm, mmm, this is good," and "Best dinner ever." Happy faces emerged all around.

Until I noticed a particularly droopy figure, hands in his pockets looking over the leaf-covered wet kitchen. Looking, but not participating. I splashed over to the tree Leon was depending on for his support. "Are you waiting for the rain to slow before fixing dinner?" I asked. Red eyes mixed with drops of rain and tears pleaded silent words.

"I know you've got to be hungry. What's wrong?" He glared toward his food bag, flatter than a stamp on a Dear John letter. This five-day trip was his first time in the wilderness, and he underestimated how many provisions he needed.

I returned his pleaful stare with a glance over to my tent. Confused, he latched on to where I was looking. Sloshing toward my corner of the campground, I reached into the food compartment of my dangling and very soggy backpack. Leon's face transformed from dread to hope as thank-you's burst forth with unabated enthusiasm. Amazing what a dinner for two can do for a hungry soul. As the leader of these city kids, I was expected to anticipate this type of situation. Nothing special there. This time I was simply prepared and could help.

Our heavenly Father anticipates our lack of food, and He is never caught off guard. I remember many decades ago talking to a cabinet builder. He was training an apprentice who moved at a snail's pace. The master craftsman turned to me and spoke words that have never left me: "I know I can work faster because I know what is right around the corner, so I can anticipate the next task. He cannot." Doesn't that describe the God of the Bible? He sees what is around the corner and knows the next step.

God was not surprised when Abraham stood before Pharaoh and distorted the truth. Neither is God stunned when we embellish the truth to make ourselves look good or put the truth on a quick diet to hide pertinent details. He made us and knows our desperate need for help.

Look with me at this strange account of God reaching out to Abraham. Genesis 15:17 sets a most peculiar stage. "When the sun had set and darkness had fallen, a smoking firepot with a blazing torch appeared and passed between the pieces" (NIV).

Understanding this verse became pivotal in my relationship with God. Such an odd verse, such a bizarre scene. Oh, but so exciting when we understand its context.

Here we go...

In those days, when kings gathered for a meeting of the minds and agreed on a certain decision, a peace treaty for instance, they sealed the agreement with a ritual. The term was to "cut covenant" where the participants pledged their lives as surety. The kings would cut a sacrificial animal in two, place the pieces on the opposing altars, and then walk in between them reciting the terms of their agreement. So God told Abraham to bring Him a heifer, a goat, and a ram, each three years old, along with a dove and a young pigeon. Abraham cut these in half, except for the dove and pigeon, and laid them out opposite each other. But only God (the blazing torch) passed through the pieces. It was a one-sided covenant.

Even if Abraham had known what was about to come to pass and would have wanted to be a part of this covenant, he couldn't have. God put him to bed. God made him tired. Abraham was sound asleep, unable to contribute anything. Only God Himself showed up. Ridiculous Mercy! He knows we are in trouble and so instead of entering into the covenant with us as participants, God takes on all responsibility. He takes care of everything!

Remember Leon? He had nothing to offer. That evening his participation at dinner was to eat, nothing else. Just like Abraham, he could only receive. God provided what he needed.

As we vacillate in our ability to trust God, we find ourselves in pretty good company. However, even though Abraham may have been kept safe each time he felt the need to come to God's rescue, there were serious consequences for the individuals he withheld the truth from, as well as his own posterity. Entire households and families fell ill. War and hatred seeped deep into feuds not yet mitigated.

Abraham faced several dire situations. Our lives are hopefully not as exciting or life-threatening, but I have a question. How does trusting God relate to a salesman who is desperate to provide for his family? Can he stretch the truth or withhold information? What do I do when my customer is an outspoken atheist? If he or she gets wind of the fact that I am a believer in Jesus, will I lose the account?

That is a possibility.

Can I trust God? Or do I tell half-truths? Answering these questions can be convicting.

I recall an incident when an employer called a friend of mine into his office for a heart-to-heart conversation. "Please pull the door shut behind you." Soft, plush carpet held up comfy, oversized chairs. The windows framed the Chicago skyline glistening after the morning rain. Beautiful, but still it felt gloomy to my friend, like being called into the principal's office all over again. His mind raced back over the past few days to remind him of all the possible things he might have messed up or missed entirely. The opening words put an immediate stop to his query. "We have a buyer for the building, and we want you to take the prospective new owners on a tour." Whew, that was not bad at all, he thought to himself.

Wrong.

Then droned the next words: "These are smart people who should know what they are purchasing, and you are not allowed to tell them about any existing issues with the building, the HVAC systems, the elevators, etc." His thoughts drifted off. There were lots of issues.

His story took my mind back to college and my own frustrations over immoral acceptable business practices. My checkbook was full of checks with very little money to back them up. I needed a car. Off to the local used car lot I went and found one that fit into my budget. The early summer heat blew through the open windows during the test drive. What a happy day. We exchanged money for the title, and I drove my new car to the dorm. Later that night a storm came up and I ran downstairs to the parking lot to roll up the windows. I turned the crank on all four doors. The dealer failed to tell me all four windows were missing.

Had the salesman told me the truth, would he have lost the sale? Possibly. One thing I know for certain. The contract he made with me was rooted in dishonesty and possibly selfishness. God's contract with Abraham, and with us, is rooted in selfless love. He offered help and a solution before we realized we needed help. Not that we deserved it. Not that we could ever pay or reimburse Him for it.

I wish I could tell you I never backed down or shied away from speaking the truth; never stretched the truth or hid it. I cannot. That also includes being transparent about my faith in Jesus. Neither is this a "Do as I say, not as I do" scenario. What I can tell you is that confessing and walking in allegiance to God becomes more natural the longer we live our life of faith. Through the years there have been, and still are, things God wants me to know, to learn. It seems, if I don't grasp it the first time, He is not in a hurry and takes me through similar circumstances again until He is satisfied. God is more interested in our growing trust in Him than He is in our temporary comfort. I realize how daunting that sounds. The only reason it should not be scary is because we know He has our best interest in mind.

Is it easy for me to confess my colors? Well, when I am in a prayer meeting or a church service, certainly it rolls off my lips. These settings are a good training ground. We receive encouragement from others through their struggles and victories. We can learn how others live their faith out loud. Hesitatingly at first, I began to speak to others outside of the church about my relationship with God, but then it became more frequent, and time was my friend. Slowly, word got out, customers and associates grew to accept my faith. I confess, there were events where they reminded me of my supposed faith and scolded me. Ugh, I had to go back, apologize and correct my behavior. I am thankful God continues to mold me into more of a reflection of Himself.

One more detail deserves attention-Abraham did not grow up in a Christian home. From what we know he was not an exceptional child. He intentionally sinned to protect himself. Not just once. At any time, he could have chosen to hang up the towel and conclude he stepped too far over the line. At any time, he could have thought he made too great a mess out of his life for God to still put up with him. There is no record, no insinuation, no hint of such thinking. Our lives may be messy, but to God, we are marvelous.

When my hopes and dreams to sing were shattered so many years ago, I was frustrated and, yes, angry. I still have CDs in the garage, memories of almost making it. I have no idea why God did not let me use the talents He, after all, had given me. Looking back, what I can see is, He wanted me to leave where I was, and move me into a different arena—just not the one I had picked. As it turned out, Lisa and I enjoy a wonderful life together, but a different life than we planned.

Trusting God is easy, as long as my plans unfold without a hitch. But trusting God is not easy when His plan for my life is not the same as mine.

Trusting Him, relinquishing control to Him, by its very definition gives Him the right to override my hopes and dreams.

But . . . He knows what is best for me.

He sees what is around the corner and looks at me with eternity in mind.

I wish I no longer doubted Him. I am still learning. Just like Abraham.

TAKEAWAYS

1. Abraham was not perfect when God made the covenant with him. Perfection not required.

2. We are His imperfect children who get to point friends and family to God.

3. God knows you and your circumstances. He is not surprised by anything.

NOTES

CHAPTER SEVEN
FILLED WITH HOPE

We began this study with the birth of our firstborn son. I stood helplessly by as complications reared their ugly head. I did not feel warm fuzzies for the doctor. He probably didn't care much for me, either. But he saved the life of our son. I was grateful.

You may have preconceived ideas about God. You might even think He doesn't like you.

Not so! He loves you.

John 3:16 is such a familiar verse. Instead of the words **world** and **whosoever**, insert your full name.

> *For God so loved _____ that He gave His only begotten Son, that _____ believes in Him should not perish but have everlasting life.*

It's true. God did this for you. And me, and a lot of other misfits.

His love is undeterred by your distrust or even current dislike of Him.

If you are not His child, He stands by the door, ready to welcome you into His Kingdom. He extends this lopsided covenant to you; He already paid it forward.

Believe.

As His child, you and I can know against the backdrop of any circumstance that He has the best view of us and longs to welcome us into Heaven.

The next few days may hold uncertainty for us. God sees our lives, in fact, all of humanity, as one great big picture. He knows what lies ahead. He is trustworthy. He sees and knows you, your struggles, failures, and strengths. He made you and loves you more than little toddlers love puppies. For now, begin to trust God for the moments just ahead of you.

Abraham was a real man, as real as you and me. Real in every way, including doubts, fears, victories, laughter, joy, anger—and the list goes on and on. He was also not a perfect man. If we were to meet Abraham in a church today, chances are he would not stand out—at all. You might ask him to grab a cup of coffee with you, and y'all would laugh, bemoan work, summer heat or winter cold, and even problems with relatives. I reckon you would notice that he has a strong sense of the nearness of God. My guess is his faith and your faith in God would naturally weave in and out of your conversation.

As we spend time with God, reading the Bible, and digging deeper into His Word, like we are doing right now, our relationship with Him grows just as Abraham's did. He wasn't a super saint. He, you, and I blunder and flourish as we make sense of God's leading in our lives. God is as committed to you as He was to Abraham and Sarah.

God sealed the deal when He cut covenant with Abraham and then with us through Jesus. God knew we could never pay for our sin and renewed the lop-sided covenant through His Son. God sacrificed Jesus, to pay for what we could never pay for: entrance into the Kingdom of God and a residence in Heaven in His presence. On the cross Jesus gave His blood for our salvation. He died, but God raised Him from the dead, and He now sits at the right hand of His Father.

I can't wait to meet you. Let's look for each other at the Marriage Supper of the Lamb!

I would love to hear your faith-story. Connect with me at RidiculousMercy. com. I enjoy reading about the ways God breaks into lives to reveal Himself.

NOTES

SELF-REFLECTION: DEVELOPING A RELATIONSHIP OF TRUST

RIGHTEOUSNESS

Then He (God) brought him (Abraham) outside and said, "Look now toward heaven, and count the stars if you are able to number them." And He said to him "So shall your descendants be.

Genesis 15:5

And he (Abraham) believed in the LORD, and He accounted it to him for righteousness.

Genesis 15:6

1. What was accounted to Abraham?

_____

_____

_____

2. When we read about his life, we see Abraham acting quite insecure about believing or trusting God. Did he grow in his ability to trust Him?

_____

_____

_____

3. Do you think you are growing in your ability to trust in God? What do you base your answer on?

_____

_____

_____

4. Is trusting others easier or more difficult than trusting God for you? Explain why or why not.

_____

_____

_____

The New Testament is consistent with this first account in Genesis.

> *And the Scripture was fulfilled which says, "Abraham believed God, and it was accounted to him for righteousness. And he was called the friend of God."*
>
> James 2:23

1. What does James say was accounted to Abraham?

_____

_____

_____

2. Why was it accounted to him?

_____

_____

_____

3. What did God call Abraham?

_____

_____

_____

The nation of Israel had not yet been born. Abraham lived more than 400 years before God gave Moses the law.

4. Was righteousness accounted to Abraham when he left his homeland in Ur?

_____

_____

_____

5. Was righteousness accounted to Abraham when he rescued Lot from the four kings in Genesis, Chapter 14?

_____

_____

_____

6. Was righteousness accounted to Abraham before or after circumcision was instituted?

_____

_____

_____

7. Did any of his actions grant him righteousness? What granted Abraham righteousness?

_____

_____

_____

8. What should we, all of history before us and all following, base our righteousness on?

_____

_____

_____

For I bear them witness that they have a zeal for God, but not according to knowledge. For they being ignorant of God's righteousness, and seeking to establish their own righteousness, have not submitted to the righteousness of God.

Romans 10:2-3

1. Is having zeal for God (living a good, moral life, etc…) sufficient to right standing with God?

_____

_____

_____

2. How do we establish our own righteousness?

_____

_____

_____

3. Can we establish our own righteousness?

_____

_____

_____

But we are all like an unclean thing, and all our righteousnesses are like filthy rags.

Isaiah 64:6

1. How does Isaiah describe us?

_____

_____

_____

2. How does he describe our attempts to be righteous?

_____

_____

_____

For He made Him who knew no sin to be sin for us, that we might become the righteousness of God in Him.

2 Corinthians 5:21

1. Who is made sin for us?

_____

_____

_____

2. Why did Jesus become sin for us?

_____

_____

_____

3. What do we contribute to this righteousness?

_____

_____

_____

SELF-RIGHTEOUSNESS

Self-righteousness is a dangerous attribute. Read the following parable Jesus told.

The Pharisee stood and prayed thus with himself, "God, I thank you, that I am not as other men are, extortioners, unjust, adulterers, or even as this tax collector. I fast twice in the week, I give tithes of all that I possess."

Luke 18:11-12

1. List the attributes the Pharisee singles out, which make him a wonderful addition to God's team.

_____

_____

_____

2. Based on these attributes, does he sound like a good man?

_____

_____

_____

3. Then what is the problem?

_____

_____

_____

4. What did he establish by comparing himself to the publican?

_____

_____

_____

5. Are we ever in danger of comparing ourselves to others, thinking we are better than them?

_____

_____

_____

MAKING PLANS

The ground of a certain rich man yielded plentifully. And he thought within himself, saying, "What shall I do, since I have no room to store my crops?" So he said, "I will do this: I will pull down my barns and build greater, and there I will store all my crops and my goods. And I will say to my soul, "Soul, you have many goods laid up for many years; take your ease; eat, drink, and be merry." But God said to him, "Fool! This night your soul will be required of you; then whose will those things be which you have provided?" So is he who lays up treasure for himself, and is not rich toward God.

Luke 12:16-21

1. Why was the rich man called to task, scorned or scolded?

_____

_____

_____

Come now, you who say, "Today or tomorrow we will go to such and such a city, spend a year there, buy and sell, and make a profit" whereas you do not know what will happen tomorrow. For what is your life? It is even a vapor that appears for a little time and then vanishes away. Instead you ought to say, "If the Lord wills, we shall live and do this or that." But now you boast in your arrogance. All such boasting is evil.

James 4:13-16

1. Do you believe it is wrong in God's sight to make plans?

_____

_____

_____

2. Is there a right way and a wrong way to plan? How do the preceding verses in James clarify our questions?

_____

_____

_____

3. What is the right way to plan?

_____

_____

_____

GOD KNOWS THE FUTURE

But He knows the way that I take.

Job 23:10a

1. Does God know where we are headed?

_____

_____

_____

2. Is He ever surprised by where we are?

_____

_____

_____

3. If He knows where we are and where we are headed, is He distant,
un-involved, removed?

_____

_____

_____

*I am God, and there is none like me, declaring the end from the beginning
and from ancient times things not yet done, saying, "My counsel shall
stand, and I will accomplish all my purpose."*

Isaiah 46:9c-10 ESV

1. Re-write this verse in your own words.

_____

_____

_____

2. If you knew the future, would you be better equipped to make decisions?

_____

_____

_____

3. Why would or should you rely on God for your future plans? Explain your answer.

_____

_____

_____

4. Do you want God to be in control of your life?

_____

_____

_____

5. Do you believe He is in control of your life?

_____

_____

_____

6. Does God see your life in sequential time or as a complete picture?

_____

_____

_____

7. Does God see the outcome of your circumstances?

_____

_____

_____

8. Knowing He sees all of your life as one, can He be a trustworthy friend?

_____

_____

_____

9. Does that knowledge instill peace in you? Why or why not?

_____

_____

_____

RELATIONSHIP - FRIENDS

One who has unreliable friends soon comes to ruin, but there is a friend who sticks closer than a brother.

Proverbs 18:24 NIV

1. Can you list reliable friends in your life?

_____

_____

_____

2. Do your friends consider you to be a reliable friend?

_____

_____

_____

3. Why do you believe they do or do not?

_____

_____

_____

4. Who is the friend who sticks closer than a brother?

_____

_____

_____

5. Are you convinced God has your best interest (eternity) at heart?

_____

_____

_____

Are You not our God, who drove out the inhabitants of this land before Your people Israel, and gave it to the descendants of Abraham Your friend forever?

2 Chronicles 20:7

1. Based on this verse, was God involved in Abraham's life? How so?

_____

_____

_____

2. Is friendship with God a fickle friendship?

_____

_____

_____

3. Do you believe Abraham knew he could lean on God?

_____

_____

_____

4. Does being called a friend of God appeal to you?

_____

_____

_____

5. What would you do, or be willing to do, to be in Abraham's place and be called a friend of God?

_____

_____

_____

Look at what Jesus tells His disciples.

No longer do I call you servants, for a servant does not know what his master is doing; but I have called you friends, for all things that I heard from My Father I have made known to you.

John 15:15

1. What does Jesus call the disciples?

_____

_____

_____

2. Does this translate to all of Jesus's servants, followers?

_____

_____

_____

3. Do you believe Jesus calls you His friend?

_____

_____

_____

RELATIONSHIP - BROTHER

Are not five sparrows sold for two copper coins? And not one of them is forgotten before God. But the very hairs of your head are all numbered. Do not fear therefore; you are of more value than many sparrows.

Luke 12:6-7

1. Do you protect what is valuable to you?

_____
_____
_____

2. Do you believe God will protect what is valuable to Him?

_____
_____
_____

3. Have you ever experienced God's protection?

_____
_____
_____

4. Have you ever thought in a fleeting moment: "Thank God that didn't happen?"

_____
_____
_____

5. Have you ever thought for just a second: "That's cool. I can't believe this just happened ... to me?"

_____
_____
_____

While Jesus was still talking to the crowd, his mother and brothers stood outside, wanting to speak to him. Someone told him, "Your mother and brothers are standing outside, wanting to speak to you." "Who is my mother, and who are my brothers?" Pointing to his disciples, he said, "Here are my mother and my brothers. For whoever does the will of my Father in heaven is my brother and sister and mother."

Matthew 12:46-50 NIV

1. Who is His brother or sister?

_____

_____

_____

2. Have you ever thought of yourself as a brother to a king?

_____

_____

_____

3. What thoughts come to mind when you pause and chew on that for a bit? Don't hurry, take your time.

_____

_____

_____

First of all, then, I urge that supplications, prayers, intercessions, and thanksgivings be made for all people, for kings and all who are in high positions, that we may lead a peaceful and quiet life, godly and dignified in every way. This is good, and it is pleasing in the sight of God our Savior, who desires all people to be saved and to come to the knowledge of the truth.

1 Timothy 2:1-4 ESV

1. What does God want for all people? (Hint: there are two answers in these verses.)

_____

_____

_____

2. What is good and pleasing to God based on the context of these verses?

_____

_____

_____

3. What thoughts do you have regarding praying for those in high positions?

_____

_____

_____

RIGHT STANDING WITH GOD

And he brought them out and said, "Sirs, what must I do to be saved?" So they said, "Believe on the Lord Jesus Christ, and you will be saved, you and your household."

Acts 16:30-31

1. How do we obtain right standing with God?

_____

_____

_____

2. At the risk of sounding simple, how are we saved (from sin)?

_____

_____

_____

3. Anything else besides believing? This is important.

_____

_____

_____

4. Do we have to "clean up" before becoming acceptable to God?

_____

_____

_____

5. Is there anything we can contribute to be saved?

_____

_____

_____

WISDOM—WHO TO TRUST

Look at this advice from Solomon, who is reckoned to be one of the wisest people of mankind. He said to his son:

> _Do not be wise in your own eyes; fear the LORD and depart from evil._
>
> Proverbs 3:7

1. What is the first step to departing from evil?

_____

_____

_____

2. What is the second step?

_____

_____

_____

3. Have you considered being wise in your own estimation to be evil?

_____

_____

_____

4. Why would it be evil?

_____

_____

_____

For I say, through the grace given to me, to everyone who is among you, not to think of himself more highly than he ought to think, but to think soberly, as God has dealt to each one a measure of faith.

Romans 12:3

1. How are we **not** to think of ourselves?

_____

_____

_____

2. How **are** we to think about ourselves?

_____

_____

_____

3. Do you believe we are good enough before God?

_____

_____

_____

Jeremiah minces no words. If we rely on ourselves or other people, well, read it out loud:

Cursed is the man who trusts in man and makes flesh his strength, whose heart departs from the LORD.

Jeremiah 17:5

1. Rewrite this verse in your words.

_____

_____

_____

2. How do you reconcile the American goal of a "self-made" man compared to Jeremiah's observation?

_____

_____

_____

3. List a few words that best describe the word **cursed** for you.

_____

_____

_____

And as it is appointed for men to die once, but after this the judgment, so Christ was offered once to bear the sins of many. To those who eagerly wait for Him He will appear a second time, apart from sin, for salvation.

Hebrews 9:27-28

1. What image comes to your mind when you hear the word judgement?

_____

_____

_____

2. We will be judged. What is the criteria for judgement?

_____

_____

_____

3. Will everybody receive a not guilty verdict? Explain your answer in complete sentences.

_____

_____

_____

4. Where will you put your trust?

_____

_____

_____

IMMANUEL—GOD WITH US

Yea, though I walk through the valley of the shadow of death, I will fear no evil; for You are with me; Your rod and Your staff, they comfort me.

Psalm 23:4

1. In this well-known verse, when we encounter serious trouble, where is God?

_____

_____

_____

2. When God slams a door shut because He sees we are just about to get into trouble, do we embrace or enjoy a sudden hook from his staff around our neck?

_____

_____

_____

3. When we walk in a direction away from God do we embrace or enjoy being prodded away from our newfound goal?

_____

_____

_____

4. Who is there by our side to do the hooking and the prodding?

_____

_____

_____

5. Nobody wants a crook around their neck. What about when we are just about to step off a ledge?

_____

_____

_____

All we like sheep have gone astray; we have turned, everyone, to his own way; and the Lord has laid on Him the iniquity of us all.

Isaiah 53:6

1. How close do we want God to be?

_____

_____

_____

2. Without Him, or even with Him, what direction are we prone to go?

_____

_____

_____

Where can I go from Your Spirit? Or where can I flee from Your presence? if I ascend into heaven, You are there; if I make my bed in hell, behold, You are there. If I take the wings of the morning, and dwell in the uttermost parts of the sea, even there Your hand shall lead me, and Your right hand shall hold me. If I say, "Surely the darkness shall fall on me" even the night shall be light about me.

Psalm 139:7-11

1. Is it possible to get away from God?

_____

_____

_____

2. Would you ever want to get away from Him?

_____

_____

_____

3. Does the knowledge that He is with you always make you feel uncomfortable? Why or why not?

_____

_____

_____

4. David says God's hand will lead and hold us. To reach us with His hand, where is He in proximity to us?

_____

_____

_____

Do you not know that you are the temple of God and that the Spirit of God dwells in you?

1 Corinthians 3:16

1. Who provides a living space for God's Spirit?

_____

_____

_____

Whoever confesses that Jesus is the Son of God, God abides in him, and he in God. And we have known and believed the love that God has for us. God is love, and he who abides in love abides in God, and God in him.

1 John 4:15-16

1. See the relationship? Where is God versus where we are?

_____

_____

_____

Therefore the Lord Himself will give you a sign: Behold, the virgin shall conceive and bear a Son, and shall call His name Immanuel.

Isaiah 7:14

Behold, the virgin shall be with child, and bear a Son, and they shall call His name Immanuel which is translated, "God with us."

Matthew 1:23

1. New and Old Testament in perfect harmony. What does the name Immanuel translated mean?

_____

_____

_____

2. Where then is God, Jesus, the Holy Spirit?

_____

_____

_____

"I am with you always, even to the end of the age. Amen."

Matthew 28:20b

1. Do you believe Jesus is with you?

_____

_____

_____

For He Himself has said, "I will never leave you nor forsake you." So we may boldly say, "The LORD is my helper; I will not fear. What can man do to me?"

Hebrews 13:5c-6

NOTES

ABOUT THE AUTHOR

Ralph Corduan is a speaker, singer/songwriter and co-founder of Ridiculous Mercy ministry. He studied music at the Munich Conservatory of Art (Germany), Oklahoma Baptist University, and the University of New Mexico. Drawn to the Church, both in the pew and outside the steeple, Ralph shares the simple message of God's Ridiculous Mercy and how He redeems and uses flawed people in the Bible as well as today.

Ralph lives in South Carolina with his wife, best friend and confidant Lisa. He is the proud parent of three sons, all grown with families of their own. And a really, really proud Opa of four grandsons and one granddaughter. Connect with me at RidiculousMercy.com.